Greenock
Then & Now
by Bill Clark

At the eastern end of Drumfrochar Road once stood the Westburn Refinery – originally built in 1896 as the Berryards Refinery. It had been taken over by Tate & Lyle in 1976, but was closed in August 1997, bringing to an end the town's over 200-year-long association with the sugar industry.

Acknowledgements

Photographs on the following pages are used with permission from the Watt Institution, Inverclyde Council: front cover, inside front cover, 16, 24, 38 & 40. Thanks to Chris Bradley for enhanced images from the Mehat collection, on pages 14 & 26, used with permission from the McLean Museum, Greenock. 'Then' photographs on pages 1, 18 & 33 were taken by Iain Nicholson. All 'Now' photographs were taken by Bill Clark, except for that on page 23, which is the work of Bill Barry.

References

Sandra Macdougal & Joy Monteith, *Greenock Place Names*, 1996.
https://www.inverclydeheritage.network/greenock
https://www.railscot.co.uk/locations/G/Greenock_Princes_Pier_2nd
https://www.jameswattdockmarina.co.uk/jwd-history.html
https://www.undiscoveredscotland.co.uk/greenock/greenock/index.html
https://www.greenocktelegraph.co.uk/opinion/14011888.flooding-chaos-of-1912
http://www.arthurlloyd.co.uk/GreenockTheatres.htm

Text © Bill Clark, 2023.
First published in the United Kingdom, 2023, reprinted 2025 by Stenlake Publishing Ltd.,
54-58 Mill Square,
Catrine, Ayrshire,
KA5 6RD

Telephone: 01290 551122
www.stenlake.co.uk

ISBN 9781840339659

The publishers regret that they cannot supply copies of any pictures featured in this book.

Introduction

The origin of the name Greenock is uncertain. The legend that it derives from a green oak tree at the edge of the Clyde at William Street, used by fishermen to tie up their boats, is generally regarded as imaginative folklore, as no reliable source has been found that references green oaks. The name is perhaps derived from the Gaelic *grainach*, meaning a sunny place, or from the Brittonic *graenag*, meaning a gravelly or sandy place. Either of these is possible, but the latter is probably the more likely, possibly originating from the associated adjective *greannach*, translating to "rough" or "gravelly". This does, indeed, describe the general nature of the ground in the area, which is composed essentially of material deposited by the River Clyde and which later became what is described geologically as a 'raised beach'. This was created when the shoreline receded as the land rebounded after the massive weight of ice overburden melted away at the end of the last Ice Age. Greenock was originally founded on this narrow strip of land, as were Port Glasgow and Gourock, backed to the south by a range of hills, stretching roughly from around Finlaystone Estate to Gourock. These probably indicate the shoreline and sea cliffs that once lined the southern side of the Clyde Estuary before the land rose.

The shore where Greenock was established originally formed a broad bay, where a safe anchorage is known to have existed as early as the 12th century. In the late 1500s, Greenock was a fishing village that sat on this bay, which became known as Sir John's Bay, when Sir John Schaw had a jetty built there. Further east, another fishing village, Cartsdyke, existed, where Saint Laurence Bay curved round towards Garvel Point. Early in the 18th century, funds were raised to extend quays out into Sir John's Bay to create a harbour. The work was completed in 1710, and in 1711 the shipbuilding industry was founded when Scott's leased ground between the harbour and the West Burn to build fishing boats. Greenock rapidly became a major port and shipbuilding centre, but also developed a significant sugar industry. By 1850, fourteen sugar refineries are recorded in operation – processing sugar cane imported from the Caribbean on up to 400 ships per year and supplying half of the UK market.

Bawhirley Road, Greenock

Many of the streets in Greenock preserve the names of once-existing farms. One such is Bawhirley Road, shown in this view dating to 1913, looking east towards East Crawfurd Street. Late 19th century maps show the farm was originally called Balwharly, but this had become Bawhirley by the time a 1905/06 Ordnance Survey map was published. This shows that the farm was situated on a track that ran west from East Crawfurd Street, some 200 metres east of where this eventually joined Kilmacolm Road – roughly where the junction with Strone Crescent is located today. The dwelling houses in the image were built on the south side of this track.

This view from Whinhill dates to between 1900 and 1910 – with many chimneys showing the industrial nature of the town at that time. The long buildings in the foreground belonged to the Greenock Ropework Company, which was founded in the early 20th century and was acquired by the Gourock Ropeworks Company, Port Glasgow, in 1936 and operated as a subsidiary company. The growth of the shipbuilding industry on the Clyde heavily influenced the prosperity of manufacturers of ropes, canvas and sailcloth, and the Ropeworks Company was to gain a worldwide reputation for its products. The works

at Greenock produced cotton fishing nets and manila trawl nets and by 1954 it had developed as a specialist unit for working in soft hemp. Today, an equivalent view, looking across the area on Drumfrochar Road now known as Broomhill, shows no trace of the former ropeworks. The image generally retains no vestiges of the town's industrial past with which to identify the original viewpoint, so it has been aligned with the distant hills.

This photo, probably dating to around 1930, shows turbine steamers *Queen Alexandra* and *King Edward* laid up for winter in the James Watt Dock. *Queen Alexandra* was built in 1912 by Denny's of Dumbarton for Turbine Steamers Ltd., to replace a previous *Queen Alexandra* of 1902, which had been extensively damaged by fire. The new Queen was designed for long distance cruises and her first commercial trip was on 23rd May 1912 to Campbeltown. Fast and manoeuvrable, she soon became a popular boat. In 1935, Turbine Steamers was sold to MacBrayne's and the *Queen Alexandra* was refitted at Lamont's

shipyard, where she was extensively modified, repainted in MacBrayne colours and renamed *Saint Columba*. She took over the "Royal Route" from Glasgow to Ardrishaig and, in 1937, became the first Clyde steamer to be converted permanently to oil fuel. Withdrawn from service in September 1958, she was towed to Smith & Houston's shipyard in Port Glasgow on 23rd December 1958 to be scrapped. Today, the former steamer dock has been transformed into the James Watt Marina.

This view looking west along the south quay shows the main feature of the dock, the Titan crane. Known as a cantilever crane, this large fitting out crane was built in 1917 by Sir William Arrol & Co. and enabled heavy items to be loaded or unloaded from cargo vessels. The 150-foot tall structure is Category A listed and is one of only a few left in Scotland (40 were built by Arrol & Co and sent all around the world). This quay runs along the front of the Sugarsheds, the corner of which is just visible on the left. The vessel at the quayside is the PS *Laguna Belle*, which was originally built as the *Southend Belle* in 1896 by

Denny's of Dumbarton for the London, Woolwich & Clacton-on-Sea Steam Boat Company. The paddle steamer served as a minesweeper in both World Wars and seems to bear wartime dazzle camouflage, so it may date to WW2. The vessel was broken up in 1946. The present-day view of the same location shows a prestigious visitor to Greenock in 2022 – the super-yacht, *Eos*, a Bermuda-rigged schooner with 200-foot masts – taller than the Titan crane.

This view, dating to the 1950s, shows the north side of the James Watt Dock, then designated Berth XXVI. This ran adjacent to the Garvel Dry Dock, which lies to the left. Beyond are buildings belonging to the British Oil and Cake Mills Company (BOCM), which was granted a lease on the site in 1920. Two years later, a mill was completed, which produced edible oils and animal feeding stuffs, using cottonseed as the chief raw material. In 1950, a refinery was built to refine linseed oil for paint and linoleum manufacturers. Today, the original viewpoint is within the dry-dock and is inaccessible because of Health

& Safety regulations. A similar angle is now only possible from the other side of the harbour looking towards the jetty from where the original picture was taken and aligned on the former coaling pier on the right. The old image shows Garvel House on the left, once used as offices, but which was allowed to fall into ruin and, despite being a listed building, was mysteriously damaged by fire one night and had to be demolished in 2004. The site is now occupied by the large blue shed, which is part of the dry-dock infrastructure.

In the latter half of the 20th century, overcrowding and poor sanitation was a major problem in the town, which was described by the Registrar-General as the 'unhealthiest town in Scotland'. The solution the town authorities decided on was to favour provision of private housing through philanthropic associations and their patrons. One of these benefactors was Sir Michael Robert Shaw-Stewart of the local Ardgowan Estate, who was the Conservative MP for Renfrewshire until 1865. He feued land at Hillend at a low rate. A row of 28 cottages were built on East Crawford Street, which were named after

his wife, Lady Octavia. In reality, most of the Octavia Cottages ended up being owned and occupied by people of higher social status than that of the working class they had been intended for. The row is shown in an image dating to 1912, with Hillend School opposite. Today, the houses still exist, but the old school has been demolished and replaced by King's Oak Primary.

A view along Belville Street in 1968 shows that demolition of the row of tenements along its north side had begun. A row of buildings appears here on maps dating back to the latter part of the 19th century, but these were replaced in the 1970s by seven high-rise blocks known as the Belville Street high flats and named after towns in the Scottish borders. Though initially popular with tenants, wear and tear was a factor, as the flat roofs were susceptible to

leaking and sloping caps had later to be fitted in an attempt to cure the problem. The flats latterly became afflicted by anti-social behaviour and crime, so people no longer wanted to live in them and they were in turn demolished between 2010 and 2014. Today, the ground remains cleared and is now the site of the Belville Community Gardens.

In 1919, the main road through the town was narrow and cluttered, as shown in this picture looking east at the junction with Knowe Road, with the Scotts shipyard buildings on the left. The yard closed in the late 1980s and the area was cleared and redeveloped, so has an open aspect, where the A8 dual carriageway now curves round towards the Cartsdyke Roundabout. The area to the right, the site of Cigna Health Care office buildings, is where a row of

buildings once stood, known as the "Lighthouse Tenements". These were built in 1705 by the Crawfurd family of Cartsburn and were originally occupied by fishermen and shipmasters of the time.

A view of Victoria Harbour in the mid-1980s shows evidence of considerable activity at that time. It then served as the port for Glenlight vessels and the local fleet of tugboats. Development of Victoria Harbour had begun in 1846, because demand for harbour accommodation had increased as the 19th century progressed and the deepening of the Clyde had generated competition from Glasgow, which had affected Greenock. The excavated material was used to fill land to the west, which eventually became the Albert Quay of the Albert Harbour, and Victoria Harbour was opened in 1850. In 1867, the Albert Harbour

was also opened, to fulfil the continually increasing demand for port facilities, but has long been filled in. Victoria Harbour remains, though it now sees little activity compared to what it did in the past. The empty skyline to the east, once dominated by the cranes of the Scott Lithgow shipyard, provides a clear illustration of the changes that have taken place in Inverclyde.

Charing Cross showing Messrs Scott's Main Shipbuilding Yard, Greenock.

A view looking east in 1912 shows the point where Rue End Street becomes Main Street. The Rue-End name does not come from the French, but is a corruption of row-end, because the end of a row of fishermen's cottages was located at this point when Greenock was a fishing village. The clock tower at Scott's yard is visible on the left but, sadly, little remains of the former shipyard – none of the buildings survive and the exact position would be hard to

determine today, but for the old dry dock. This is just out of view to the left, so by aligning on this it becomes possible to work out that the Cartsburn Roundabout now occupies this location. The area where the shipyard once stood is occupied by an EE Customer Centre, a Holiday Inn Express and a Royal Bank of Scotland office building.

A postcard dating to 1905 shows the original St. Laurence's Church, which stood at the corner of Rue End Street and Dellingburn Street. The church, which is documented as the first religious building in Scotland to use electric power, was destroyed during the Greenock Blitz, when multiple waves of German aircraft bombed the town on the nights of 6th and 7th May 1941. The building, a Gothic design by London architects Pugin and Pugin, was burned out

after the air raid, leaving only the baptistry intact. The church was never rebuilt but was replaced by a new building on Kilmacolm Road, which was opened in 1954. During the 1960s a fire station was built on the original site, replacing the previous station within the Municipal Buildings, which is now a museum.

An image from 1919 shows an impressive building standing in Wallace Place, with a small garden area leading up to the front. This lies between the western facade of the Municipal Buildings and the area of the town on the right, then known as the Vennel. This building, originally built around 1881, served as the main Post Office until 1899, when it was replaced by new premises on Cathcart Street. It was then purchased using a donation made by Scottish-American

philanthropist Andrew Carnegie and converted into a free public library. Carnegie performed the opening ceremony on 10th October 1902. As he had done with all the libraries he helped create, he asked for a 'Let there be Light' inscription to be placed above a 'sunburst' glass pane over the entrance. The building still exists and today it once more serves as the Central Library but, sadly, the Carnegie entrance features are gone, as is the garden area.

This view from 1968 looks across Hamilton Street towards Wallace Place, down what was once known as Taylor's Close, running along the side of the Central Library building at the centre of the image. Hamilton Street, which once ran from Cathcart Square to Westburn Street, no longer exists, having disappeared when this section of the town was redeveloped as a shopping centre in the 1980s. As part of this redevelopment, a new Central Library was

built on Clyde Square, but the old building survived to serve as the Council Rent Office. However, in 2015 it was restored to its former use, once again becoming the Central Library. It is now largely obscured from the original angle by the north-eastern corner of the shopping centre, which was roofed over in the 1990s and became known as the Oak Mall. In 2023, however, a proposal is in place to demolish this part of the mall and relocate the eastern entrance.

The foundation stone for Holmscroft School was laid on 28th February 1887, in the presence of civic leaders and members of the Greenock Burgh School Board, on the site at the junction of Dempster Street and Ann Street. The school was described as a new type of building with a simplified form of Gothic design, and the first in the area laid out with a system of sliding partitions allowing the whole upper floor to be converted into one hall for meetings. In March 1966, when the premises functioned as the Holmscroft Annexe of the Watt College, the roof caught fire. The building was subsequently demolished in 1968. A sealed lead box was discovered above the door on Ann Street, which had been placed there during the laying of the foundation stone. In addition

to a copy of the *Greenock Telegraph*, the contents included papers relating to the functions of the school board, guidance for teachers and rules and regulations to be followed. The site is now part of the footprint of Greenock Health Centre, which became functional in May/June 2021. This occupies the area stretching up Ann Street from Wellington Street to Dempster Street, where the South Parish Church and the school formerly stood. The present-day photo shows the rear of the building.

Looking towards the junction with Inverkip Street is the west end of Roxburgh Street in 1916. Previously known as Alexander Street, the street was renamed after the Roxburgh Estate in Tobago, owned by Archibald Shaw-Stewart, a son of one of the major local land-owners. In the latter part of the 19th century, the Roxburgh Street Refining Company was one of the many that operated sugar refineries in the town. A present-day image shows that much change has

taken place here over the past century. The tenements on the left appear to be original, and the red sandstone block on the right, at the corner of Newton Street, has survived, but the adjacent buildings have been replaced by a modern apartment block. Where a row of shops once stood is now a car park.

In 1807, funds were raised to build a hospital or infirmary on a site on the east side of Inverkip Street. The foundation stone was laid in 1808 and it opened in June 1809 as a voluntary hospital funded by subscriptions, providing 32 beds. Additional ground was provided in 1815 to provide a larger airing ground and two wings were added in 1830. By the mid-1840s capacity had been increased to around 100 beds. It was extended onto East Shaw Street in 1847, and in 1869 a new building was added on an adjacent site in Duncan Street. The hospital is shown in 1906. It was renamed Greenock Royal Infirmary in 1922 and joined the NHS in 1948, but closed in 1979 when Inverclyde Royal Hospital opened. The buildings were demolished and the sheltered housing complex for seniors, visible in the present-day image, looking up along West Shaw Street, was opened in 1988. This was named John Galt House, commemorating the novelist and entrepreneur who was buried in the adjacent Inverkip Street Cemetery in 1839.

This view from 1986 along West Shaw Street, up towards Inverkip Street, shows Walker's sugar refinery. Founded in 1826 this was managed under various ownerships until eventually being purchased by John Walker & Co. around 1850. In the 1950s, it was taken over by the Tate & Lyle Co. and operated until 1979, when the refinery closed. In the distance, on the other side of Inverkip Street is the Royal Infirmary, which was demolished in the 1980s and replaced by the Sheltered Housing Complex, John Galt House. Today, the roads have been realigned, so that West Shaw Street is no longer a through route, and the area between Inverkip Street and Nicholson Street is largely occupied by retail businesses.

The aftermath of a deluge that engulfed Greenock in 1912. On Monday, 5th August, a heavy cloudburst caused torrents of water to plough through the town. Culverts on the West Burn became blocked and the Murdieston Dam overflowed. The water poured down the steep streets into the cutting of the Glasgow and South Western Railway line and rushed through the tunnel leading to Princes Pier, flooded the sidings above Brougham Street and spilled over, damaging tenements on either side of the bridge. Rescue operations had to be established and people were evacuated, some having to be lowered

from first floor windows using knotted bed-sheets. Rescue facilities were set up in the Picture Palace, which was undamaged. The picture shows people queuing on Brougham Street to be fed there. The incident subsequently caused lawsuits to be raised by the railway companies, which were decided in their favour, and set precedent for the law on culverts. Formerly a roller-skating rink, the Picture Palace had opened as a cinema in 1912 but closed in 1929, when the Gaumont was opened, and then became a ballroom. The premises are now occupied by a snooker hall and a restaurant.

West Blackhall Street was, and is, one of the main shopping streets in the town. Like several of the streets in Greenock, it takes its name from an estate – in this case, the Blackhall Estate, in the Paisley parish, which belonged to the Shaw-Stewart family. This view, which appears to date to before the First World War, is looking west from the junction with Westburn Street. This was once on the main route through the town, with a tramway that ran along Brougham Street, Grey

Place and West Blackhall Street. At this point, the trams continued onto Hamilton Street, but this street disappeared with the building of the Oak Mall Shopping Centre, which opened in 1992. The present-day image has been taken from near the mall's western entrance. Much change has taken place at this end of the street and none of the nearer buildings seem to have survived, but some of those more distant are recognisable and serve to positively identify the location.

Near the centre of this 1919 view of the top end of West Blackhall Street stands the Hippodrome. This building opened in December 1858 as the new Theatre Royal, but in 1905 it became the Palace vaudeville theatre. This was planned to be managed together with the nearby King's (formerly Alexandra) Theatre, the edge of which is visible on the left, but by the following year plans had changed and it was renamed again, this time to the Pavilion Theatre. In 1908 the theatre was re-modelled to become the Hippodrome Theatre of Varieties. This eventually closed on 1st December 1923 and the building was scheduled

for demolition to make way for re-development. It remained empty for six years and was demolished in 1930. A present-day view can be aligned on surviving buildings further along and shows that the sculpture of "Egeria the Wood Nymph" now stands where the Hippodrome was and the new road that was extended from Grey Place, to connect with and extend Dalrymple Street, runs through the former sites of the Waverley Temperance Hotel and the King's Theatre (latterly the Odeon Cinema).

Old maps show that Crawfurd Street was once much longer – running parallel to West Blackhall Street, across Laird Street and Nicholson Street, as far as Westburn Street. When the road system was changed to bypass the town centre by extending Dalrymple Street west to Grey Place, most of Crawfurd Street disappeared, leaving only the western part shown in this photograph from 1919. A present-day equivalent from the corner of Hood Street (once known as Nelson Street) shows mostly industrial businesses, including the *Greenock Telegraph* office. On the right of the old image is the junction with York Street,

which once led to Clarence Street but no longer exists. Beyond that, at the corner with Ker Street, is the former Glebe Sugar Refinery – one of the last surviving remnants of the once-thriving sugar industry. The five-storey building was a later extension to the original sugarhouse built on the other side of Ker Street in 1831. A bid was made by Inverclyde Council in 2023 to obtain finance from the Levelling Up Fund for the regeneration of the town centre, which included a proposal to convert the Glebe building into a new cultural centre.

In December 1869 the Caledonian Railway was bypassed by the rival Greenock and Ayrshire Railway, which opened a station on the waterfront, served by a tunnel under Greenock's west end. This was the terminus of a line running between Glasgow St. Enoch and Greenock, via Kilmacolm. The service connected directly with the Clyde steamers, which the Caledonian service did not at the time, as it terminated at Greenock Central. The station was originally called Albert Harbour, but was renamed Princes Pier in May 1875. The original station was replaced by a new station in May 1894, and this is

shown in 1938, taken from the Esplanade. The station had four canopied platforms and the three exits had towers on each side, presenting an impressive sight from the river. Following the post-war decline in rail use, regular passenger services to Princes Pier ceased beyond Kilmacolm in February 1959, and the station was closed to freight in 1966. It was demolished in 1967 and the site, along with the in-filled Albert Harbour, is now part of Greenock Ocean Terminal, the container gantry cranes of which are visible in the present-day view.

The Royal West of Scotland Boat Club at the western end of Greenock Esplanade seen in 1907. This was founded in 1866 by the owners of houses along the Esplanade since, as a result of its construction, they had lost direct access to the river and needed somewhere to keep and launch boats from. They formed the West of Scotland Amateur Boat Club and constructed the clubhouse. In 1885 the Club was granted the Royal Charter after providing a boat that was used to row Queen Victoria on Loch Maree, during one of her summer tours of the Highlands. The clubhouse itself has changed little, but the

surrounding area has seen some major changes. Behind to the right, on the site of the old Fort Matilda coastal battery, once stood the local office of the Maritime and Coastguard Agency, known locally as the Admiralty Building, which was home to the Royal Naval Reserve training centre, HMS *Dalriada*, until the end of September 2012. Following closure of coastguard facilities by the MoD, the property was sold and the buildings were demolished. Apartment blocks have since been constructed on the site.

In 1907, under an Admiralty compulsory purchase order, the Royal Naval Torpedo Factory (RNTF) was constructed, as the principal centre of torpedo production in Britain, on land to the west of the old coastal battery at Fort Matilda, between the Esplanade and Battery Park. The RNTF opened between 1910 and 1912, employing 700 workers transferred from Woolwich, and the original picture appears to date to shortly after the opening. During the 1960s, the factory took part in the top secret Project Chevaline, intended to improve the survivability of Britain's Polaris missile against anti-ballistic missile

(ABM) systems. Completed in 1969, this was the final project, following which the factory closed and remaining work was transferred to Weymouth. During the 1980s, the eastern end was demolished to make way for residential development, as shown by the present-day image. Since the original viewpoint is now impossible to access, this has been taken from about the same angle but from higher ground. The western end was developed as Fort Matilda industrial estate and still contains a number of original RNTF buildings, which were assigned listed building status by Historic Scotland in 2006.

Spango Valley seems to have taken its name from a shortened form of Spangock – one of the three lands belonging to John Schaw, which were formed into the parish of Greenock shortly after the Reformation. IBM opened a factory in the valley in 1954, on the site of the former Kingston Farm, and an aerial picture dating to the 1980s shows the once-thriving manufacturing plant, at the time when road re-alignment and conversion to a dual carriageway was in progress. The plant gradually expanded along the valley floor, eventually extending to about a mile in length. Much of this was taken up by the Materials Distribution Centre (MDC), an automated warehouse visible on the left of the earlier photograph. This was demolished in 2009, then the remaining buildings were sold and partially leased back, but the site was finally vacated by IBM in 2016. A view dating to October 2018, taken from just below the Greenock Cut from roughly the same angle, shows a completely empty site, so all the buildings that existed in the 1980s had been demolished by then.